New Pair of Shoes

"Coloured Bedtime StoryBook"

By

Boutsakone Somphanthabansouk

Illustrated by

Bounpheng Chanthavong

ILLUSTRATED & PUBLISHED
BY
E-KİTAP PROJESİ & CHEAPEST BOOKS

www.cheapestboooks.com

 www.facebook.com/EKitapProjesi

ISBN: -978-625-6308-96-1

Copyright, 2024 by e-Kitap Projesi

Istanbul

Categories: Problem Solving
Country of Origin: LaoS People's Democratic Republic
Cover: © Cheapest Books
License: CC-BY-4.0

For full terms of use and attribution, http://creativecommons.org/licenses/by/4.0/

Contributing: Bounpheng Chanthavong

© **All rights reserved.**

Except for the conditions stated in the License, no part of this book shall be reproduced or transmitted in any form or by any means, electronic or mechanical, including photocopy, recording or by any information or retrieval system, without written permission form the publisher.

About the Book

The rain makes the road muddy, so Khamla slips, and tears his shoe. What should he do? Will he get new shoes?

New Pair of Shoes
Boutsakone Somphanthabansouk
Bounpheng Chanthavong

After school, Khamla walked home.

It suddenly rained making the road muddy.

Khamla slipped and tore his shoe.

When he arrived home, Khamla told his mom, "Mom! My shoe tore. I want new shoes."

Mom said, "I don't have money to buy you new shoes."

"I will ask Dad!" says Khamla

Dad said, "Let me see if I can help. Let's sell our vegetables at the market this Saturday!"

Khamla said, "I'm so happy! I'm going to get new shoes soon!"

After school on Friday, Khamla helped his mom and dad collect vegetables from the neighbors to sell at the market.

Khamla and his parents packed the vegetables in a cart.

The next morning, Khamla and his parents pushed the cart to the market.

"Vegetables for sale! Fresh vegetables! Organic vegetables!"

After not too long, they had sold all the vegetables.

They were so happy to earn money from selling the vegetables.

After that, Mom bought new shoes for Khamla.

On Monday morning, Khamla happily wore his new shoes to school.

End of the Story

www.ingramcontent.com/pod-product-compliance
Lightning Source LLC
LaVergne TN
LVHW070454080526
838202LV00035B/2831